THIS DAY IS DARK

ALSO BY R.H. SIN

THIS DAY IS DARK

r.h. Sin

Andrews McMeel
PUBLISHING®

ACKNOWLEDGMENTS

To Samantha, my wife, thank you for being one of the happiest places I've ever been.

INTRODUCTION

Where is the beginning of the pain, the trauma, and the emotional anguish? I think if I'm being honest, the troubles, my troubles, began long before I ever thought to record them in writing. This story, or the fragments of darkness, began when I was small and before my mind could suppress the fragmented tragedies of my existence. I decided in my teens to jot down the days of darkness in a composition book. I'm a bit of a futurist, and when I began to publish my thoughts on the internet using a few aliases, and at times under my real name, that composition book would find a new home in a folder on each laptop I owned. The very first home was a mini Acer laptop. It was blue—I hate the color blue—but it was all I could afford after being forced into homelessness. I was living in an old car that I bought with cash, and that little laptop had seen its fair share of drama as it fought to survive being crushed and later thrown in an attempt to be destroyed by someone I thought I could trust. In fact, some of the entries were shared across my first three bestsellers, *Whiskey Words & a Shovel* volumes 1–3.

What you read here is a journey into the past, the beginnings of an active volcano that has threatened to erupt fully over the course of my life. What you will consume here is a record of all the days that made me question my life, my choices, and the direction I've headed in.

Currently, my wife is in the living room with our children, and I'm in the office writing this before I put our youngest down for a nap, and in so many ways, this feels like a goodbye. This book itself feels like a goodbye letter to my readers, but, in fact, this is me burying all the pain and trauma. Not in a way of suppressing or ignoring it, but a proper goodbye, an honoring of the lessons that I've learned from the dark.

I sometimes think we as people take a bad situation and make it worse by what we hold on to mentally; we get into our heads and hurt our hearts even more. We overthink, we lose control, we feel lost, and we end up broken. Here is a record of all the times I've deemed dark, and by the end of this, I'd like to say goodbye to everything that hurt me. I'd also like to say thank you to every moment that broke my heart because, in the end, I grew stronger.

I have to put my daughter down for a nap, but I hope the words in this book speak to you, and maybe they'll mean something different for you from what they meant for me. Whatever the case, I hope this book touches your heart, because it definitely touched mine as I wrote it.

In remembrance of all the days we have felt like we weren't good enough and to all the mornings we rose, only to discover that we are stronger than before. *This Day Is Dark* is dedicated to you and me.

THE NOISE

in crowded spaces
I am embraced
by the cold arms of loneliness
the sun is shining
but there's a rainstorm in my heart
my head hanging low
I see my reflection in a puddle
sad, tired eyes looking back at me
as if I were a stranger
my lover doesn't love me
proof of this is in their absence
standing in front of me
still miles away
plotting ways to leave me
but only when they've found a replacement
no one just says it's over
you only know it
when their attention is thoroughly enthralled
by the next person
no one tells you the love is gone
they just continue to say I love you
but their ways are hateful
all this is one day; this day is dark

goodbye dances
on the tip of my tongue
but I remained tight-lipped
in hopes of change
I've been waiting in the rain
dark clouds sit on top of my head
like a hat made of misery
you promised to meet me here
you vowed to, remember
December, where we met
then near the ocean
face-to-face
I've run out of apologies
you don't take accountability
how did our peaceful home
become a war zone of tension
and why does
our love story
haunt me

before you tell the world
about what you found wrong with me
be sure to also mention
that of all the friends and family you had and have
I was the only one who meant it

the yelling changes nothing
remaining calm changes nothing
being silent makes it worse
preparing to let go
because nothing seems to work
I'm out of words
I'm out of hurt
I've grown numb
to every moment
I've felt this for a while
but you've been too busy to notice
I've felt this since a child
because my mother was the same
and I was bound to repeat the cycle
trauma bonds are to blame

There's always that moment when you realize that you no longer fit into that person's life; that's when you begin to drift in the opposite direction. That interest you were able to maintain becomes weaker, and, slowly but surely, the feelings fade.

I think some of us just have a higher threshold for heartache, and so each blow to the chest pushes us closer to the edge of moving on, but just because you can take the pain doesn't make it hurt any less.

Have you ever noticed how the person in the relationship who rarely shows up always believes themselves to be the prize? All you ask of them is to do the most basic shit, and they fail you time and time again as they pretend that you will be losing something. In this person's head, there is a strange belief that even as they are not actively adding anything to your life, somehow if either of you decides to leave, you'd be losing something. Or even worse, they see themselves as the victim, and every time you open up to say what you need, they're also in need of something you're already willing to give; they're just not present enough to receive it.

I know you've been there, struggling in the dark, silent because you don't know whom to trust or who will listen, and because I've been there before, I can understand everything that you may be feeling, maybe at this exact moment. I hate to see you break down, but I do want to see your breakthrough, and sometimes it takes falling apart to discover that part of you that is strong enough to walk away.

sometimes the answer
to all your questions
can be found
in the way
they remain silent

The person who pisses you off has no right to tell you what to do with that anger.

People are not elevators. You can't push a person's buttons and then dictate their direction. So often, a narcissist will do everything in their power to upset you and then play the victim if and when you blow up or lose it. Keep a watchful eye on anyone who wishes for rain and then complains about the storm.

You're not perfect; there's nothing wrong with you; you're not crazy or angry or any of the things a narcissist attempts to label you. That reaction you had the other day results from your heart being tired, but even better than expressing that anger, perhaps it's time to let them go.

there are nights when
my mind feels full
and my heart feels weak
there are nights when
I collapse into myself
as the memories of what we were
weigh heavily on my shoulders
there are moments under the moon
in the darkness when I struggle
to find the power to forget about you

I kept waiting for this to make sense; I'd chosen you for a reason, but we've been in hell together for so long that the answers left in heaven are much harder to find. I don't even know the way back to bliss, our peaceful beginnings replaced with fire in the form of yelling—our actions toward one another symbolic of all loss of respect.

How is it that you can get it completely wrong? How is it that your love feels like hatred most of the time, and how is it that your well-wishes often lead to a moment when you're just pulling me down or keeping me stuck? I matter, but I don't. You want me to be happy, but I can't. You'd like me to stay, but every action causes a reaction where I'm forced to consider leaving. Somehow you need me, while half the time, I feel unwanted. I don't understand how you fail to comprehend the fact that your words don't line up with your actions.

too often
and too long
I've invested
the right type of energy
into someone committed
to treating me wrong

death has been
kinder to me
than you'll ever be
giving me chances
you'll never give
extending me grace
you denied me

they always forget
the things they loved about you
they always forget
the way you showed up
for them, while the rest of the world
watched them struggle
they always forget
until it's too late
then they remember
and remember
then remember
until they themselves
are only a memory

sometimes they wait
until the end
to value you
and rarely should that
ever be enough
to keep you

the sooner
you reach for the end
the sooner
something better
can start

Eventually, you learn that words are often used as masks and that the best way to get to know someone is not by talking but by spending time with them and observing what and who they truly are.

I wish sleep was as easy as turning out the light.
I lie here in the dark, cold, incapable of warmth,
staring into the gray corner, wondering how my
life became a rainstorm when all I longed for
were rays of sunshine.

it's hard to enjoy the sun
when there's a storm
growing in your chest

You know what, when your nights become flushed with restlessness and winter comes early to your heart. When you are weighed down by confusion, the betrayal becomes a constant fixture in the spaces where you desire the complete truth. I hope you learn to use your fire to set yourself free. I genuinely believe relationships don't have to be complicated, and I hate the way you've been forced to think that you are asking for too much when asking for the bare minimum. Love doesn't have to hurt; pain does not have to result from love.

I think you and I have struggled in our desire to be with someone who is ready and willing to match the effort we give. I think you and I have fought to be seen and heard, only to be misunderstood. I've been where you are many times, and I have made several discoveries on that journey that I intend to share with you. I myself have enjoyed the beautiful embers that dance away from the flames of the bridges I've burned, and I hope she finds this, she being you. I hope you learn to enjoy the fire and the fact that you are capable of creating your own flames.

I hope you remember
everything they never knew
how I sacrificed my dreams
so that yours could come true
how I championed your name
when you lacked self-belief
pushed you to become more
of what they said
you'd never be
I hope you remember
all the things you'll never share
how I always stayed close
never strayed, always there
now I'm the bad guy
of course, so convenient
I thought I was your home
until you decided to leave it
let's make one thing clear
this shit is over
because of you
relentless and persistent
in all the things
you put me through
all I wanted was love
but I guess it ran out
I just hope you tell them
the truth
whenever you feel like
running your mouth

isn't it wild
the way your heart
can become homesick
for a place
that doesn't appreciate
your very presence

being left alone
with my mind
can be dangerous
this grief is sharp
the sadness
slices through me
from within

wouldn't the end
be sweeter
if you had the choice
of choosing
what memories stay
and what could be
forgotten
you spent the entire relationship
swearing you loved me
and when I decided
that leaving would be best
you spent the better part
of our demise
filling the time with hate

you can't nurture a rock
you don't water a stone
no amount of love
will soften the heart
of a person
who doesn't intend
to love you

when you've
been in pain
for years
"it gets better"
sounds like a lie

most of the time
being half loved
light kisses
and weak hugs
"I love you"
sounds so empty
"I miss you"
your favorite lie

too young for the love I seek
too old for the games
you've been playing with me

today, I don't have the strength
to hide this sadness
today, you'll see a storm inside of me

Nothing I've loved has been able to remain in my life. Whether by force or natural circumstance. I lose everything I give my heart to.

you got hurt
because you confused
obsession with love

we were torn at the seams
once, we came together
and now we're falling apart

I feel everything
even when it's nothing
my heart is heavy
even when it's empty

Sometimes two people need to fall apart because they were never meant to come together.

Maybe hell is just another name for the people who make the decision to hurt us.

sometimes your pain inspires me
I cry your tears while writing down
the things you've kept inside

It's hard to leave when you haven't a place to go.

I wasn't yelling to overpower or hurt you. I screamed because that was the only way I could force the words out.

the commonalities were a lie
we are nothing alike

I'm not trying to hurt you. And I'm sorry that my desire to be happy has caused you pain.

You spend months, maybe years, pretending to be happy with the relationship you settled for because, deep down, you believe things will get better or at least go back to how they once were.

the more you ignore the wound
the wider it grows, the deeper it gets

healing is a silent home
a lonely path, an empty road
people rarely see your wounds
and despite the pain, you feel
you spend most days forcing a smile

We always talk about soulmates and their association with true love, but we never talk about soulmates who aren't prepared to love you correctly. A thing that is "meant" to be won't always happen.

Even her silence sounded sad.

I can't say that I'm entirely healed, but I'm not mad anymore; I just can't look at you the same.

you took too much
and rarely gave

slowly, I can feel you letting go
but you keep me, just in case
claiming to love me
while searching for my replacement

it hurt so bad, I smiled
nervously looking up
into a dark sky
gathering with black clouds
waiting for hail to fall
while lying in hell beside you

there are no bandages
strong enough to drape over
the wounds of heartbreak
no magic word
to chase the pain away
you have to sit in it
that chair made of misery
in the middle of the room
surrounded by
cracked paint and mold
you have to face it
until your pain is faceless
you have to struggle
to get to the other side
love comes unexpected
but so is the trouble behind it
the painful moments that drown out
the sound of every beautiful promise
love arrives when you're not looking for it
but so do the pain and disappointment
I couldn't see it
no, I wouldn't see it
I tried my hardest to believe in a lie
and in place of love
is this gaping hole inside my heart
a void where you used to be

our relationship rendered lifeless
I try my hardest to move on
but it's hard to kill
what is already dead

the red flags
look like the color of passion
and love being waved toward the sky
when you're blinded by your feelings
things done intentionally
get called mistakes
"I'm sorry" is a quick fix
a way to speed up forgiveness
even when that person doesn't mean it
forevers are temporary
"I love you" is just a routine lie
and "I miss you"
is a roadblock
to keep you from moving on
this is what you learn
from loving the wrong people

if you won't love me
let someone else try
I cry toward the heavens
tired of this hell
I've waited around
you didn't show
I've repeated your name
and still no answer
you don't love me anymore
you just hate the idea
of me loving someone else
or that someone else
could love me more than you did
if you can't love me
set me free

the optimism is denial
I've been forcing myself
to think positive
despite negative feelings
I keep building bridges
instead of a boat
I continue to make excuses
to smother the truth
you don't even have to lie to me
I've been lying to myself
afraid to open my eyes
I choose to remain ignorant
this is the fear of starting over

what will you remember
when I'm gone
the sad song of our troubles
or the melodic laughter
that formed a bridge between us

the record player kept skipping
I could hear it but couldn't move
there was thunder and lightning
but I just sat silently
beneath that dark cloud
I saw people running
but I just stood there
frozen in time
afraid but stuck
a fire began
the smoke detector screamed
the dirty air filled my lungs
but I wouldn't leave
that burning house
this is how it feels to stay
with someone who is committed
to their desire to hurt you

It wasn't a question as to why you can't love me; what I should be concerned with is why I even care.

We were supposed to be a team, but you treated me like competition.

Quietly noticing everything. Saying nothing is so fucking painful.

people rarely see your wounds
and despite the pain, you feel
you spend most days forcing a smile

You've been searching for salvation in the person who only causes you pain. Stop.

How could you call this love when it resembles hell?

You're not afraid to lose me; your only fear is that I'll find someone first.

Our love became a wound.

you're toxic
I have to stop
breathing you in

what was once
sweet to taste
is now bitter fruit

drunk off your potential
and promises
I stumbled into hell
believing it was love

we're like a poem
running out of words
losing its meaning

forever is something we say
but it's never what we do

tired of handing roses
to the person
who treats me like weeds

I'm nowhere near perfect, but I tried for you. I tried for you even though I knew it wouldn't make a difference.

every ache in my body
is a story of how
you saw the world
on my shoulders
and decided not to help

I'm confused because this is not the forever you promised. This is not as timeless as I once believed. I've been sitting in this dark room trying to see it for what it is. I was living in color but now I'm unhappy in gray.

I'm tired.
I'm tired of asking you for something
you're not willing to give.
I'm tired of working on myself
while you refuse to make the necessary changes
to make this work.
I'm tired of trying when I see no real effort.
I'm tired of fighting for someone
who only wants to combat everything I say or do.
I'm tired of loving someone who acts like they hate me.
I'm tired of trying to talk like adults while you act like a child.
I'm tired of sharing my feelings with someone
who is offended by the pain in my heart.
And so, this silence is not a way to get you back.
It is not an attempt to hurt you.
My silence is a decision to save my words
for someone who wants to listen . . .
because fuck you, fuck this. I'm tired.

Sometimes the person you love is incapable of loving you the way you deserve. Sometimes the person you want doesn't deserve your devotion. Sometimes the person you fall for doesn't dare to fall beside you. You can't continue fighting for someone who doesn't have the energy and time to want to work on the relationship. You can't expect it to work when the other person has decided to do something else or, worse, look to someone else for all the things you were willing to give.

The worst thing about an ex is that sometimes they stand in front of someone better, distracting you with a false sense of hope.

me, never witnessing love
growing up
I almost believed
I'd witness it with you

if we could start over
I would have never wanted to know
about all the bodies you chose
before placing your fingertips into my skin
if we could start over
I'd take more time
to know you on my own
instead of relying
on your past
to paint the picture of you

you're not
the same person
I fell for
you're not even
a better version
it's like you walked backward
only to transform
into someone I've never met

waiting for someone to change
when they see nothing wrong
with how they hurt you
is a self-destructive hope

I stayed awake
to make the night longer
because I knew
I'd be gone in the morning
we had all the time in the world
and lost it
love would not see us
through another day

she was beautiful on the surface
but I couldn't help but feel
that there was a terrible
feeling of sadness
bubbling beneath her skin

She was loved in words but never in action. This is why she was so sad.

They're always telling her how beautiful she is,
and still, they put her through the ugliest shit.

he said anyone
would be lucky to have her
yet he left her . . .

being with him
didn't stop her
from being lonely

He wasn't giving you space during the argument; he said nothing and left because he didn't give a fuck about what you were feeling.

the painful parts
are all hidden away
the words to describe
this pain are a secret
I guess this is why
no one knows
afraid to burden others
the fear of being judged
claiming everything is fine
feeding the illusion
while starving the heart
of what it actually wants

you do things
you don't want to
out of loneliness
their warm body
is never enough
to chase the cold away
lying beside them
feels lonely
and when they kiss you
goodbye
the sentiment
is always empty
but you repeat the cycle
knowing damn well
these interactions
will never settle
the sadness in your soul
I'm not judging you
I just want you to know
that you are not alone
I see you

grief
is the price I'll pay
for loving someone
who wasn't prepared
to love me back

it's like the silence
got louder
it drowned out
all the things
we should have said
to one another

it is critical
and most difficult
to find someone
who will love you
when you're sad
and running on empty

perhaps it was foolish
to believe
that I could build
a happy home
when every house
I've known was broken

I wish I knew
what love looks like
I'm tired of trusting
my deceiving eyes
my parents denied me
those lessons
the only examples shown
were anger and disgust
pain and deceit
and every moment after
the chapters
have all been the same
here I am once more
writing a book about pain

how many times
will forever be cut short
how is it that a lifetime of love
ends prematurely
you spend the rest of the time
thinking about what could have been
questioning what went wrong
and you move forward
without an answer

I've been sifting
through the madness
of our relationship
searching for my heart
and the courage
to walk away

I saved everyone else
from drowning
but when I look up
from the sea
those people
are nowhere
to be found

sometimes growth
is not enough
to keep a person
sometimes growth
is the very reason
you lose that person

I want love
the thing is
it's just hard
to find someone
who wants it with me

it's difficult
the way they claim
to be in love with you
then quietly
they change their mind

four walls
of false security
a place to sleep
eat, bathe, and fuck
but all my life
I have never
been home
and I am still searching

you're not in love with me
you're just afraid to be alone
and I am the cure

the thing about an attractive person
they hide disaster so well
you see beauty
instead of trouble
even the devil
can wear a handsome face

the way I choose a person
sometimes I think
I'm attracted to loneliness

being with the wrong person
shatters your perception of self
so much so
you look into a mirror
and see a stranger on most days

dancing alone
to silent drums
you hear a song
meant only
for the loneliest of souls

foolish to believe
that because you know
far too well
what it feels
to be abandoned
you could never
leave me
but you did

the most difficult thing
is being left behind
by someone who stands
beside you physically
but is elsewhere emotionally

when I needed you most
you offered me nothing
but your absence

I love you
but never enough
to want you back

I get upset
with my fellow man
and the way
they're willing to lose
a magical woman
how do you begin
to crush a flower
whose only wish
was to bloom

I realized the other night
that I had spent
our relationship
praising you for what
I hoped you'd be
instead of who you were
and I'm sorry
for being more in love
with my fantasy
instead of your truth

I lost you
to your ambitions
because your dreams
had no room for me

letting go
doesn't mean forgetting
moving on
is a decision
to cultivate the future
despite a painful past

the heart breaks
and you survive
in a million little pieces

I believed you changed all this time, but maybe this was who you were the entire time, and it had to get dark for me to see the light.

so often, I silenced my peace of mind
for the chaos that was loving you

the problem had always been
you weren't afraid to lose me
and so you did

you act like
you're the best I can do
while treating me
like shit
we're both confused
you exaggerate
your importance
and I pretend
that you love me

our love, a ghost
the story of you and me
a haunting tale
of what happens
when two people
fall out of a love
that was supposed
to last forever

I miss my mother
the woman before
not after
the one from the beginning
the one who would have never
allowed it to end the way it did
I miss her protection
her watchful eyes
guarding me
I've spent the majority
of my adult life
feeling like a kid
stuck in a rainstorm
without an umbrella

I guess we built our friendship
out of wood instead of steel
you set fire to your side
and that was the end
of you and me

they often care
when it's too late
they want to help
when you've outgrown
that need for assistance
oh, how I wish
they could see the pain
in the eyes
of smiling faces
oh, how I wish
they could see me
for what I feel
instead of how
I pretend to be

doesn't it hurt
that painful realization
that the wounds and scars
were not of the enemy
or a stranger
the pain which
you've been dealt the most
has often come from those
you've loved the most

it sucks being alone
when you're with
the one you love

for years
I've told myself
that it gets better
and there are moments
when I feel
the optimism
is the pain

still trying each day
to heal from the things
that you didn't think
to apologize for
still fighting to forgive you
though you were never sorry

I'm sorry, you see love
where there is only hell
your feet, they ache
you've danced
with the devil himself

I wonder
how far
must I wander
to get closer
to you
it's terrible
this feeling
of never knowing
what to do
my troubles
have doubled
it's heavy
I break
I cry
and stumble
thinking
how much more
can I take

I wish love wasn't seasonal
the kind I need
doesn't seem to need me

it's hard to move on
when they refuse to tell you
whether or not it's actually over
you cling to the hope
for change
as they quietly search
for someone new
to replace you with

never make a person
feel like you love them
when you don't
never let a person
feel like you don't love them
when you still do

long gone
before you ever noticed
too far gone
to ever come back
it happens over time
but you never see it coming
the forecast read sunny
but here, it only rains

when it ended
I didn't lose a friend
we'd been enemies
far before we'd chosen
to go our separate ways

you're still fighting demons
you'll never acknowledge out loud
still trying to heal from things
you refuse to talk about

I've been trying to figure out if there is a sort of sleep for the soul because I've been tired, rendered restless beneath a full blood moon, and I don't think closing my eyes for an extended amount of time will fix the weariness that lives in my chest.

playing melancholy songs
just adds fuel to my sorrow
music is both the sickness
and the cure

people ask if you're okay
I wish people asked
are you sad instead

when something hurts your heart
you're the quietest you've ever been
how can one ask for help
when pain causes silence

it's sad
to think about . . .
but oftentimes
the ones who
ask how you're doing
are the same ones
who don't intend
to be there for you
when or if
you're falling apart
it's like asking
is just a thing to do
and actually being there
is just too much

depression
is a body
trying to fight
while attached
to a mind
that feels like giving up

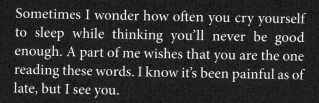

Sometimes I wonder how often you cry yourself to sleep while thinking you'll never be good enough. A part of me wishes that you are the one reading these words. I know it's been painful as of late, but I see you.

I know that choosing peace means losing you, and I'm fine with that because I've given you so many chances to be better.

I see you pretending that you're okay with your current situation out of fear of being disappointed, but behind all the bullshit is someone who wants to be chosen by the right person.

For once, I'd like to be loved entirely and consistently.

I'm so tired of moving on
my soul has grown weary
from all my attempts
to push forward
without the person
I thought I needed

sitting in a corner
wearing a mask
unable to breathe
a few feet
in front of me
my newborn
staring into space
an alien
in a strange land
so full of life
while I'm weakened
by a virus
that enjoys death
she, at the start
of her own life
watching her father
nearly lose his

somewhere, someone is wasting their grief
heart in a million pieces
for a person who wanted nothing more
than to see them break

I carried hell with me
because I refused
to let go of your hand

well, I'd chosen
to ignore it
but the pain
never left

less than
hurried
alone
and weary
these are the things
you made me feel
while loving you

it's like our book
ran out of words
or maybe there weren't
enough pages
for us to continue writing

my loved one's stare
has so much hate in it
claiming to care
and I just pretend to believe it

The frustration is a sign. The way you force yourself into silence whenever they upset you is a sign. Listen.

I sit in the silence
of my misery
trying to figure out
where we went wrong
your ghost
still follows me at night
saying nothing
staring at me
with dead eyes
static in your movement
chained to me
is the regret
of allowing you
into my heart
I struggle daily
to force you out

a break
that can't be fixed
a heart
that won't recover
a love
begins to fade
a warmth
becoming cold

the problem with potential
is that you don't use yours
this could have been more
but you didn't allow it to grow

Sometimes you envy the people who are good at smiling during moments of hell, but I don't think you understand how beautiful it is that you are willing to cry and visibly break when your world has been flipped inside out. Your honesty is inspiring.

It is truly exhausting to spend most days at war with your brain. That battle is unforgiven. Those are the moments I wouldn't wish on anyone.

filled with heartache
with nowhere
to place my troubles
I am carrying doubt
disappointment and sadness
around like a limb

let you tell it
I've given up on you
but you don't see
the moments when
I'd reach for you
in search of support
and you were nowhere
to be found
holding my hand loosely
kissing me lightly
quickly leaving my embrace
with no desire to be held
and no intent to love me back
you were sitting beside me
the entire time
but refused to hear
my screams
so now that this is over
I hope you're honest with yourself
I don't care about what you tell others
as long as you see the truth
instead of a lie
that helps you avoid
accountability

there's this troubling
thought I have
or maybe it's more so
a fear of mine
but I do wish
that I could open up
to someone
without feeling
like a burden

the pain
the heartbreak
the disappointment
the uneasiness
and the tension
that follows
all of these things
will make sense to you
when it is time
it's just not time yet

I sit here alone
surrounded by souls
suffering in silence
from things
no one will know
trying to grow
without nurture
in a drought
with no rain
struggling
to go unchanged
but I'll never
be the same
my heart's wound
got much larger
larger than expected
I tried so hard
not knowing
I'd be neglected
I thought I'd be enough
but my all was rendered nothing
who knew you could feel unwanted
in a relationship
where you also feel stuck

I've been losing sleep
wearily moving through
my thoughts
restlessly overthinking
wondering if this
will ever change

your actions
numbed everything
inside me but the grief
how can I feel nothing
but somehow
suffer from every bit
of sadness in my heart

I'm haunted
because each day
I live with the ghost
of everything
you used to be

for years
in silence
I've been
surviving myself
unable to sleep
hoping to make it
to the morning

all my secrets
live at midnight
everything
I keep from people
I tell it to the moon

I'm burned out
the flame you see
is just an illusion
something you've created
to best help you
ignore and avoid
the elephant in the room

how do you even begin
to tell someone
what is wrong
when even you're struggling
to make sense of it
yourself

you don't hear me
because everything
I have to say
is not something
you care to hear

will you love me this way
or as much as you claim
when I've decided to leave
or will my desire to be at peace
without you
reveal the hate you have for me
when you know it's truly over

I'm starting to lose the part of me that wished you'd treat me better, and that alone makes me happy.

I left to end the nightmare
I left because I needed to dream

where you were once made of glass
your heart turned to stone
you just needed to protect yourself
it's not your fault

when shit gets dark
you find your light

the rain will purify your heart
the flood will wash away
what shouldn't stay
the storms will make you stronger

sometimes you have to lose people
so that you can see
how powerful you can be
without them

the loss of you
is a chance
to gain all the things
you denied to me

people leave
they walk away
they move on
and so will you

each year is a page
in your book
keep reading
it gets better

relationships die
so that love
can be renewed
and given unto self

there's a lesson in the lows
there is wisdom in the fall
let this pain teach you
let this heartache
show you what you're made of

she didn't fear the darkness
the stardust in her bones
meant that she was at one
with the midnight sky

sometimes a relationship has to end
to keep you from sharing parts of yourself
with someone who doesn't deserve
everything inside your heart

you will struggle with self-love
until you learn how to forgive yourself

the people who hurt you
are teaching you who to avoid

Your relationship spoiled a long time ago. Why do you insist on keeping something past its expiration date?

It's completely fine for others to heavily lean on me, but when I need to lean just a little, it's a problem. This is why people like us rarely ask for help.

I'm tired of endings
you're tired of starting over

you have to understand this . . .
I almost died twice in the last 3 years
on each occasion, there was a newborn
in the other room while I was fighting to breathe
and I think the very thought of my babies
helped me find new life
whenever I look into my children's eyes
I see the saviors of my life
and it's funny because as they may raise hell
in the midst of the chaos and noise
they are still my angels
I love them to death
as they have loved me back to life
I dreamed of you last night
it's the same dream it's always been
you stretching your hands from heaven
because you know how tired I get
your eyes begin to water
because you know I won't go
I still have business here
still wish to watch my children grow

as a child
I was afraid
of Father's Day
a day to reflect on
how lonely my heart had become
not having my father to hold me
when I needed him
I wish I didn't miss the chance
to be loved, protected, and taught
by the man who gave me his name
and I wish he tried harder to be there
his absence lives with me
as I fight to be to my kids
what my father
could not be to me
Happy Father's Day, Dad
the kid in me who you abandoned
still loves you

the apologies are out of fear
you were never sorry
until you looked me in the eyes
and realized that I was finished
the apologies come too late
"I'm sorry" should never be
the last resort
"I'm sorry" should never be the thing
to save a relationship
that had been ending for years
I wish you cared this much
when I told you what I was feeling
and now your interest
in fighting for this
comes when I'm too tired
to keep trying

you're good at replacing people
I know this because I
was the replacement
for someone else
I am to become like
the people you left
or left you
before, it was my turn
to be loved, neglected
and discarded

r.h. Sin

maybe you never cared
and I just made you feel important
until my efforts were no longer enough

first, silence
then the sound
of the heart, breaking
darkness smothers
the room
then morning
becomes the cure
and light begins
to find its way to you
this day has been dark
and midnight is heavy
but come morning
you find the will
to begin again

there are prisons
built beautifully
to look like love
cages disguising
themselves
as relationships
lovers
who hide hate
in their heart
we romanticize
the pain
we tell ourselves
that this is what happens
when the heart decides to feel
we lie to ourselves
to remain in spaces
where true love
will never thrive
you can't live a life of peace
when the person you're with
is the reason you're dying inside

meet me in darkness
I long to see your light
show me your scars
I want to marvel
at your survival

that was the issue
I tried to hold you
in my hands
when you could only fit
inside my heart
I kept you on my mind
not knowing that your home
was inside my soul

for the poet
words stir tirelessly
in the soul
voices from within
scream in search
of a way out
in need of a place to land
a desire to live on paper
this is why I'm writing to you

there are wars
rumbling inside my chest
but I'm too much
of an introvert
to show you these troubles

I have forgiven people
I'll never be able to trust again

you made me feel like an obstacle
you made me feel like
I was standing in the way
of something better

what we had
and what we lost
were two entirely
different things
who you were
in the beginning
could not compare
to who you became

I'm sorry for expecting
you to be able
to return the effort
you asked me to give

THIS DAY IS DARK

tired of being treated
like a park
you visit for fun
then return home
as if we never happened

the distance
it didn't bother me
it was the silence
that destroyed
whatever we were
trying to build

part of surviving
is pretending you don't care
I won't judge you
I understand

you don't have to be sorry
for the way you decided
to heal and fix all the things
that they attempted to destroy

open your eyes
when you're in love
don't confuse real life
for the dream you've had
see the person you're with
define them by their actions
and not their potential

if it keeps you drowning
in rivers of sadness
it is not love

we're always looking forward
at the bridges we built
but don't be afraid to burn
the ones that wait behind you
it is necessary to set fire
to any road the past can take
to get closer to you

lingered on the clock as I'd become aware that we were almost out of time. Tomorrow would never know us; midnight would mark the end. I watched you inch closer to a door I wouldn't be able to use because I knew you'd lock it behind you, and I didn't have the key. One day it'll make sense, but right now, I'm so confused.

I expected your eyes
to always light up
at even the thought of me
imagine the pain I felt
to feel overlooked by you

how could something
so happy
become the reason
for eternal grief
look how quickly
our river of love
ran dry

my mother let go
of my hands too early
she left me in the deep end
unaware if I could swim
she forced me into winter
shoved me out into the cold
without a coat
I watched her turn her back
with no remorse
without care
this is why I'll never trust you
or anyone else
because my first true love
the woman who
brought me into the world
couldn't care less
if I could survive

you collapse into yourself
when you have no one
to run to
you sit quietly
when breaking
for fear of being judged
for what you're feeling

my trauma didn't make me stronger
my trauma taught me
that opening up makes me weak
my trauma taught me to hide myself
for fear of being abandoned
so no, I will not thank abuse
and punishment
for making me a better person
nor will I ever be grateful
for the act of being beaten
for the sake of being
a disciplined individual

when a parent
gives you the bare minimum
but claims it as their best
when a parent
blames not knowing better
instead of wanting to learn
to actually be better
when a parent
punishes you
for your imperfections
but can't take criticism
in the areas where
they failed you
when a parent
just wants you to get over it
without even saying sorry

I stopped being upset with you
when I met your family
my closure and resolve
were in being able to comprehend
who a person is destined to become
when raised in a toxic environment

time is the bare minimum
truth is the bare minimum
human decency
is the bare minimum
if my requests
for the bare minimum
are a burden to you
please get the fuck
out of my life

I could never be
good enough to my mother
one mistake would render me
a piece of shit
and every act of kindness
was never enough
to remove the clouds
she'd assigned to hover
above my head
it rained
when I deserved the sun
I hurt myself
trying to make her happy

the disaster and chaos
in this world
are no surprise to me
for I was raised
in a home
that was rarely
accommodating to me
or my needs
my peace of mind
challenged
during my entire youth
the world hasn't gone to shit
for those of us
who were in hell
the entire time

spending your life
searching for an escape
is not living at all

your existence
is a revolutionary act
even when the people you love
make you feel less than ordinary

just because
heaven is difficult
to find
doesn't mean
you should settle for hell

our stars
belong
to different
constellations
we are not meant
to shine side by side

you never mean
to hurt me
but you never intend
to protect me either

funny
the way
the fear
of losing
someone
forces you
into actions
that will push
that person away

you're a daydreaming insomniac
the days are filled with fantasy
the restless evenings are a nightmare

false prophets
sound honest
when your heart
is breaking

you hurt me more
as a memory
than you did
when we were together

four walls
a roof
a bed
but no sleep
eyes close
weary soul
a nightmare
I can't dream
tired and left behind
distant and broken
regretful because
somehow, this is what
I've chosen

the narcissist will calm you
just to make you vulnerable
and unprepared for the terror
they wish to inflict

I am tired
from every moment
I chose to invest energy
into pleasing the people
who have always made me feel
as if my efforts were never enough
weary from all the sleep I lost
staying up late to think of ways
to make you love me
not knowing you never could

we cry
because sometimes
the hurt can't be lifted
with words
we cry
because sometimes
the only exit for the pain
is through our eyes

to hell with them
feed the anguish
to the flames
free yourself
from this pain

kept from the truth
so long you start lying
learning the ways
of those who hurt you
you become like
the people you hate
telling yourself the same lies
they tell you

it hurts to know
that this wall
I'm building
will also make it harder
for love to get in
but I'd rather take my chances
than let you back into my life

a tree must lose
its leaves to survive
the loss makes room
for something new
to grow

I don't think I'll ever fall in love again. I'd gladly
walk to it next time.

you don't really want me to stay
you just hate the idea
of losing me to someone
you think might be better
than you are

love grows the longer you feed it
and now that we are at our end
the size of what we cultivated
is beginning to crush me

you can't cultivate peace
with the same friends
who get excited about drama
you can't elevate
with people
who can't stomach
the idea of you
being better
you will never heal
surrounding yourself
with people
who desire the tea
made from your trauma

you've been waiting for them
to change for years
but nothing came
rain in place of sunshine
hate in place of joy

sometimes I think
I needed to suffer
I was incapable
of truly seeing you
up until the moment
I could no longer manage
to pretend to be okay
with all the bullshit

you figure out
how to fly
when the ground
beneath you is destroyed
thank you for the land mines
I found my wings
because of you

I'm just trying
to separate
pain from love
I just want to be able to fall
without worrying about
where I'll land
tired of endings
tired of confusion
tired of being hurt
by the person
who promised
to be different

I know I have to be present
but it's nice to think
that each tomorrow
the moments in the future
are without mistakes and regret
it's nice to know
that there is a day
waiting for me
that is without
the pain
I've gotten used to

"it's okay"
is a mean thing
to say to yourself
when you're obviously
in pain and disappointed

it's so difficult
to motivate yourself
to walk away
when your heart
isn't sure about leaving
it's so difficult
to move forward
when the person
you needed
has decided
to finally be
what you dreamed
it's so difficult
to leave
when leaving
would unleash hell

here's the thing
that may be difficult
for you to grasp
and ultimately
your reaction to me
needing to leave you
in order to be happy
will tell me everything
I need to know
about what you truly feel
but sometimes, loving someone
means letting them go
especially when
you made them feel unwanted

was it really love
if what I felt for you
was based purely
on the picture
I created of you
in my head

the way you think of him
isn't the way he is
you keep saying you're in love
but there's a sadness in your eyes
you keep saying he's the one
but even as you read this
you're unsure

she's still grappling
with the fear of losing herself
in the event of falling in love again
love itself doesn't scare her
it's the idea that she can end up
back in a space
she's fought
to free herself from

you can't let
how it was
keep you
from realizing
how things
have become

know the difference between
being showered with love
and smothered by it
one feels toxic
the other
feels like a remedy

you must never shrink yourself
to shrink yourself
to fit inside their heart

you keep telling me
there's no one like you
and my God, I hope
that's true
because my heart
was once a river
and you forced me
into a drought

we edit
the memories
so that they
won't hurt
as much

heartache is a passage
toward learning
the pain itself
is just a dreadful lesson
going through hell
will teach your heart
to recognize heaven
when the gates open

the friends who turn out
to be enemies in hiding
are fascinating unimaginable horrors
that you never see coming

your problem is
you like to pretend
that you're okay
with losing me
and your panic
and disbelief
in me abruptly leaving
are too late and never enough
I wish you cared this much
when I was willing
to fight for it
you show up
when it's over
begging for us to survive
a death that happened
long ago

don't look for the sun
in a place where it is raining
do not search for warmth
in a space built to be cold

for some time
what we've created
has begun to break down
each day
the cracks in our foundation
become larger
greater and more difficult
to ignore
we're so much closer
to falling apart
nowhere near
where we need to be
to hold this thing together
and I accept that

the distance between
waiting and moving on
is far too close
and extremely miserable

you're a part of me
and even that realization
doesn't keep me
from regretting you
I can't look you in the eye
can't stand your presence
it's almost as if
I'm trying to break up
with myself
it's so fucking hard
because it feels like
I'm trying to leave me

that girl
loves too deeply
for those who never
have the intention
of loving anyone else
that girl has a heart
that deserves to be appreciated
and yet, so far
it has only been broken
and I wish she knew
just how valuable
she'll always remain
even when others fail
to acknowledge it

a million times
she tried
and now it's over
for good

it's easier said than done
but she's getting better at it

she fell as if
to find comfort on the floor
silently screaming to herself
broken up by the betrayal
she deserves love
but all she's ever known is pain

you know sometimes
you're lonely for so long
that you choose being wanted
over being with someone
who deserves your presence
I understand

alone she sat
beneath a half-moon
full of remembrance
for everything
she needed to forget

she stopped fighting
arguing was no longer
an option
the fear of leaving
seemed less intimidating
you did your best
to hurt her
but she stopped reacting
she'd been walking away from you
and she didn't even know it yet

now and then
there is good
in goodbye
now and then
a chance to rejoice
in the end

we kept going
but the truth is
this ended
some time ago

I know love
can be dangerous
but will you make it safe
I know love
can be wild
may I be free
with you

I gave you my best
even as you treated me badly
I gave you love
in exchange for hate
I was willing to forgive you
even when you were never sorry
and so I walk away
knowing I tried my best to stay

she started to remember
what it felt to be truly loved
the moment she walked away
from the wrong person
only to return to herself

attention is not love
being wanted
can't compare
to being deserved
and or needed
lust will never be enough
never make the mistake
of choosing temporary
over what is destined to last
stop chasing what won't be yours
stop pursuing someone
who treats you like a secondary option
do not pick a partner when you're lonely
fall in love when you've healed
and be mindful of who you decide
to create your memories with

I missed the old us
and hated what we became

soft skin
tough heart
sad eyes
but she smiles
I know what you're hiding
it hurts, but you won't say it

calm when she needed to be
a storm when it was time
a woman is everything
you are transformative

I stare into
the saddest parts
of her heart
and there I witness
roses grow

she is trying her best
to enjoy being alone
without those familiar
feelings of loneliness
this is her chance
to heal

I feel what you're feeling
I am where you are
you're the color blue
a hue of sadness
a heart that breaks
from within
I feel like you feel
I'm here beside you
our wounds identical
the shape of heartache
in our chest
while melancholy music
plays in the background

it hurts
I get upset
I'm mad
I raise my voice
I yell, I scream
I'm pissed
it's a cycle
nothing changes
nothing fucking changes
my voice begins to fade
my fucking voice begins to fade
I'm running out of words
I'm running out of patience
I begin to internalize this shit
I begin to speak only to myself
the voices from within
overpower the urge to speak out
I get silent; you hear nothing
and then I'm done; I'm gone
I leave; it never fails

I don't want clouds of hope
don't tell me it's going to get better
I want rain; I want hail
I'll sit through tumultuous weather
and if my brain is filled with doubt
let me be; let it hurt
I need to sit on these thoughts
wondering why it didn't work
I don't need motivation
I'm tired of that compromise
I don't need a fucking shield
I need to see the fucking lies
I stare at my own reflection
like what the fuck happened to you
traumatized and disappointed
to the point I can no longer move

I want the heartache
that follows
the truth's a hard pill
to swallow
how I go from
filled with love
to broken and hollow
the tough times
the dark days
the painful conclusion
a heart filled with regret
and the fear of what I'm losing
the fear of ending something
afraid of starting over
maybe I can smile again
when this dark day is over